MW01628724
Letter
YOUR
F✌CKING
heart out!
Beginner lettering & modern
calligraphy for crafty ass bitches

Want free goodies?
Email us at lettering@honeybadgercoloring.com

@HoneyBadgerColoring

@Honey Badger Coloring

Shop our other books at
www.honeybadgercoloring.com

Wholesale distribution through Ingram Content Group
www.ingramcontent.com/publishers/distribution/wholesale

For questions and customer service, email us at
support@honeybadgercoloring.com

Like free shit? Who doesn't?!

Before we jump into this motherfucker – check out:

www.honeybadgercoloring.com/freeshit

Sign up for our lettering newsletter. By joining, you'll get some super sweet shit including practice pages from the book (strokes, alphabets, words, connectors and additional projects), as well as more dope lettering goodies, tips and tricks, and freebies that all crafty bitches will love!

TABLE OF MOTHERFUCKING CONTENTS

[are you fucking
ready to letter!?]

STRIKE A POSE: POSTURE

Not gonna lie to you, posture, pen grip, and paper position can be pretty damn hard when you're starting out. So, whether you are right-handed or left-handed, remember that you're a crafty bitch and you can get this done!

Let's start with the easy shit of how to position your body and hold your pen.

You're probably like, "why the hell should I care about body??" After all, you're not in fucking elementary school anymore. Don't worry, you'll be super grateful later that you did. When lettering, the movement of your pen is incredibly fucking important. If you want to be in control of your movement properly, then you have to make damn sure that your body is positioned in a way that you can see all that you're doing and have a full fucking range of motion. But if you wanna do it right, you can't be lettering while shaking your ass. Instead, you'll have to sit at a table or a desk, with both feet flat on the ground while sitting straight-ish. No need to act like a stiff fucking robot, just relax and sit up without hunching over your paper. Try to keep the forearm of your hand lightly resting on the table and use the other hand to keep your damn paper stabilized. With lettering, you gotta move your entire fucking arm to make the fluid stokes, as opposed to only your hand and wrist. This provides your crafty-ass a greater range of motion and control over the stroke itself.

PEN

When holding your pen (or whatever fucking lettering tool you're using), you want a moderate grip on the pen – think firm enough that you have steady control, but loose enough that your strokes flow naturally as hell. Make sure your grip isn't too far away from the tip of the pen, or you won't have amazeballs self-control. And last, but certainly not least, when holding a brush pen, it's all about the damn angle. A brush pen is essentially a marker that has a flexible tip, and if you try writing with the pen tip straight down, you aren't getting any of the benefits of that flexible tip, bitch! By holding the pen at an angle, you are able to make the thin upstrokes and thick downstrokes, depending on how much pressure your ass decides to apply!

As you work on the practice strokes that you'll find later in the book, you'll start to get a real fucking feel for it. Don't stop doing practice drills until you find a grip, body position, and paper placement that make the strokes feel natural as hell and not forced. Calm down and be patient thought – this is a new type of muscle memory you're trying to learn, and it's gonna take some time.

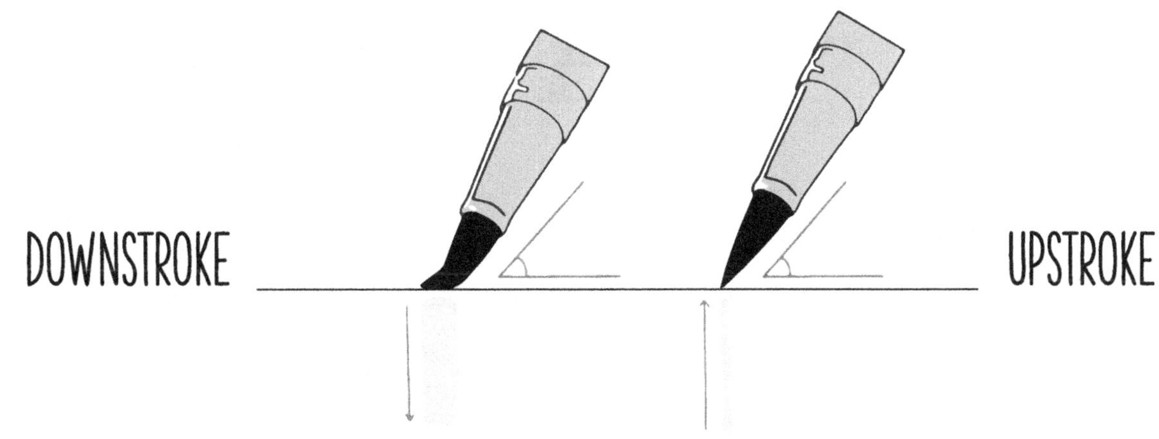

YPOGRAPHY FOR BASIC BITCHES

The best way to approach hand lettering is to quit fucking thinking about lettering as just writing words. Instead, start thinking about it as drawing words. Just like you need to understand anatomy when drawing a person, it's equally important as hell to understand the anatomy of letters when you're lettering!

Here are some of the most basic bitch terms that you'll want to familiarize yourself with before you go any further, so that as you draw each letter and word, you know how each of these elements come together to create your final beautiful fucking design. You're gonna keep seeing these terms throughout the book so make sure you study up!

The baseline is the damn line where the letters rest.

a

baseline

The midline (also fucking known as the meanline) is the line in between the baseline and the cap height.

midline

The ascender is the upward vertical stroke in letters such as H, B and K. Easy shit so far, right?

h

ascender

The descender is the part of the lowercase letters such as G,J,Q,P and Y that extends below the damn baseline.

g

descender

The serif is the cute, little, tiny-ass extra stroke found at the end of the main strokes of the letter (the little feet).

A

serif

Sans Serif means a letter sans (without) the extra stroke (footless).

A

san serif

The downstroke is the part of the letter that you push down to make (harder pressure for thicker lines).

downstrok

The upstroke is that sassy part of the letter that you move your pen up to make (light fucking pressure or thinner lines).

upstroke

The cross stroke is like totally the bar that crosses through your letter, such as in A,H,F, and lowercase T.

cross stroke

A flourish is an exagerrated swash, found on the first and last letters of a word or letters with ascenders or descenders. Got it?

flourish

A swash is a slightly extended serif (essentially, a flourish with a little less damn whimsy).

swash

N'T BE A TOOL: USE THESE TOOLS

One of the coolest parts about lettering is that there are damn near limitless options when it comes to styles, tools and techniques.

Here are some super basic bitch styles for reference:

monoline

[TOOL: ROUND, HARD TIPPED MARKER OR PEN]

For monoline lettering, the line width is consistent through the entire letter. Basically, you can have a thick-ass line, or you can have a super thin line, but, bitch, you can't have both! Monoline letter is easier to start with since you use consistent pressure throughout the entire word (don't worry – no need to change your pressure between upstrokes and fucking downstrokes).

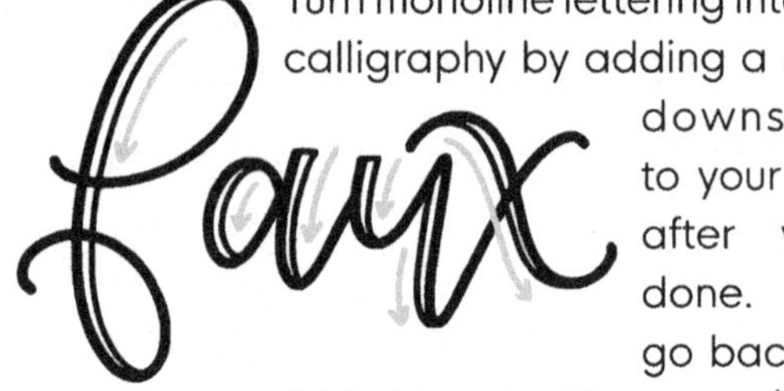

Turn monoline lettering into faux calligraphy by adding a bonus downstroke to your word after you're done. Then, go back and fill in those fucking gaps (or you can be a bad bitch and leave them as is)!

brush

[TOOL: BRUSH PEN]

For brush lettering (aka Mondern Calligraphy), you use a brush pen (or a paintbrush, or a marker with a flexible tip) and you apply some hard pressure with your downstrokes and light pressure with your damn upstrokes. It can be tough to get it down right away, but you're a crafty-ass bitch and with enough practice you'll have it mastered in no-time! Just make sure you use high quality, or heavy weight paper when using your brush pen, since you need the movement to be super smooth without the damn brush snagging on the paper fibers.

Use a water brush (or a rounded watercolor brush – whatever floats your freaking boat) to do your brush lettering with watercolors! This is a bit more difficult to master, so try starting with a small brush tip. You can bet your ass that a small brush tip is easier to control!

water

traditional

[TOOL: TRADITIONAL POINTED PEN WITH NIB]

With traditional calligraphy, you use a pointed pen (often a wooden or plastic handle with a metal nib attached) and an ink well. You can also use traditional calligraphy « pens », which are pens with the hard tip with a slanted point. Traditional calligraphy is very structed and follows some pretty damn old-school standard rules with regard to letter height, spacing, placement, etc. Because it can be very difficult to learn, and therefore frustrating as hell for someone who is just starting out, you can just stick to the whimsical monoline and brush styles in this book because fewer rules means way more fucking fun!

CHOOSE YOUR FUCKING WEAPON

HELL YES. ART. SUPPLIES.

Get ready to spend your entire paycheck on art supplies, bitches. Let's be honest, lettering can quickly spiral into an expensive hobby pretty fucking quickly. But you have to remember that at the end of the day, all you really need is a solid pencil and piece of paper to make some incredibly cool shit.

☞ **Pencils.** Sure, it's simple and basic. But let's be honest, so are most fucking people. The pencil is great way to sketch your design before going over it with a pen or a marker. Whether it's a wooden #2 or mechanical, a pencil is always a damn solid option.

☞ **Pens.** Don't know what the fuck you're supposed to use for monoline lettering? Try a pen, baby! Micron pens are notoriously smooth as hell and will look great! You can even switch your shit up by using gel pens or felt tip pens.

☞ **BrushPens.** Brush pens will become your latest obsession super fucking quickly. With so many to choose from, try testing a few out to see which one best fits your vibe. While it's going to take you a hella long time to master, don't give up. Avoid starting with a larger and softer brush pen because they can be shitty to control when you're just starting out.

☞ **Watercolors.** You bet your ass you're going to love playing around with watercolors. Whether you're using a small watercolor brush or a water brush pen – feel free to get experimental and have a blast lettering with these beauties.

☞ **Chalk.** Who the fuck letters with chalk? You will. Chalk pens are extremely satisfying to letter with and end up looking amazeballs.

☞ **PointedPens.** Pointed pens are the damn pens you picture in your head when you think of traditional calligraphy. They're pretty shitty to start out with so maybe save them until you're no longer a newbie.

☞ **Paper.** Don't forget about one of the most important parts! The damn paper itself! You'll need some high-quality paper if you want to have smooth, fluid strokes. Cheap, shitty paper is not only annoying but can actually damage your brush pens! So, make sure you spring for the good stuff for your real projects while you practice on printer paper!

BASIC BITCH STROKES

g exciting! Now you finally get to do the damn thing and put pen to paper. Even though thick and thin strokes for when you're brush lettering, this is still great practice if you're using a pen or pencil. Once you're done with these basic bitch strokes you'll have mastered all of the elements you need to for letters and words. Just focus your shit on applying consistent pressure and focus on your strokes!

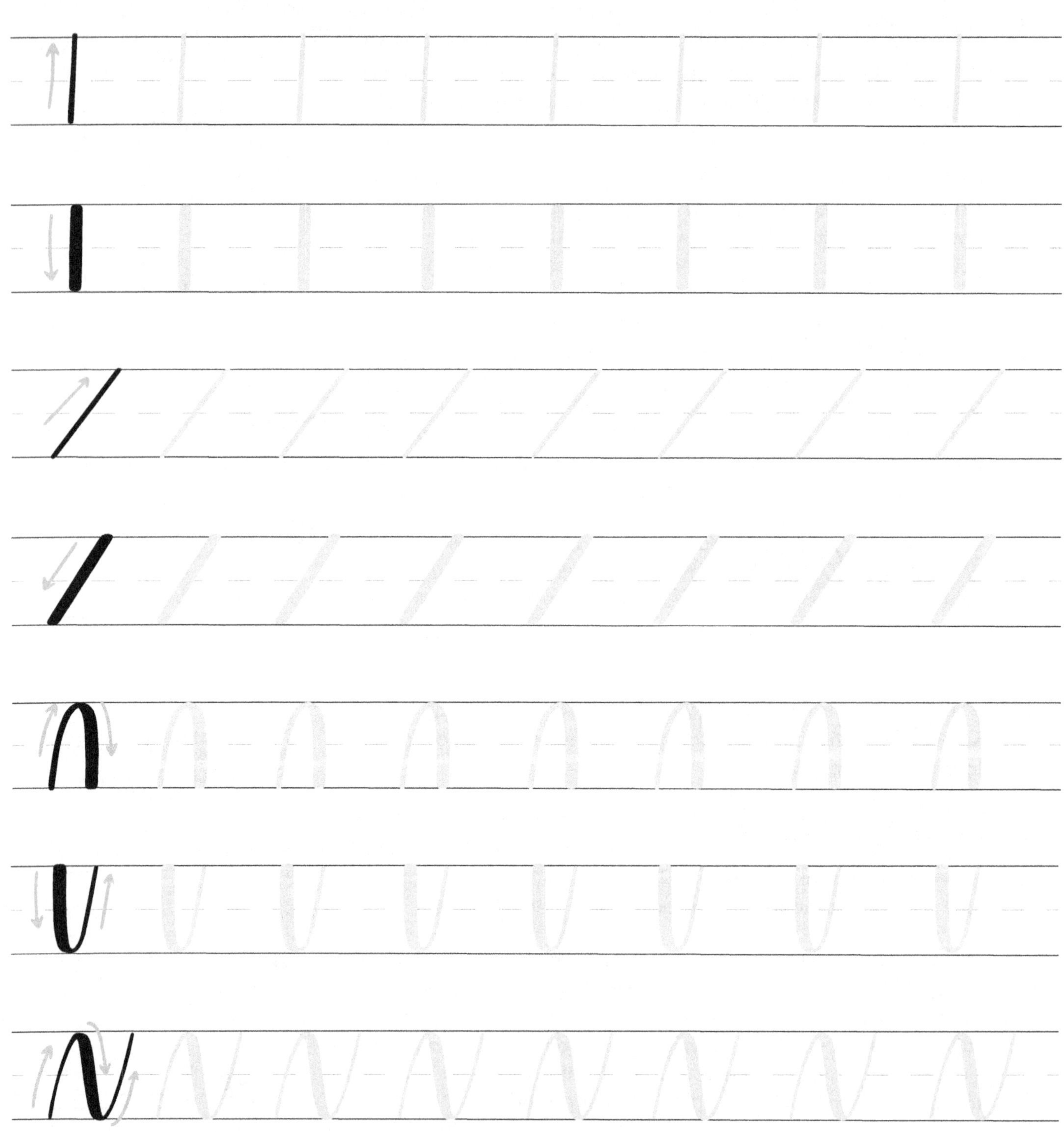

Hey! Friendly reminder to use light fucking pressure for upstrokes and use hard fucking pressure for downstrokes.

BASIC BITCH STROKES

o

l

lll

lele

m

w

l

f

PRACTICE YOUR STROKES

DON'T FUCKING GIVE UP! KEEP PRACTICING!

While your strokes won't be perfect yet, don't forget that you're a fucking boss-ass-bitch! Wanna master your strokes and build that sweet-ass muscle memory? After you finish the practice drills you can try using some of the super sick free printable downloads!

PRACTICE YOUR FUCKING LETTERS

Let's be honest, lettering is fucking hard if you go too fast. Take a chill pill and pick up your pen after each STROKE. Now, don't pick up your pen after each damn letter, but each stroke. This is where all of your fucking awesome muscle memory comes into play after all of the strokes you just practiced. Study each and every damn letter below and break them down into individual strokes. Bitch, it's gonna be hard to break your old habits from cursive, but don't worry. If you catch yourself writing a whole word without stopping, remind yourself to take a damn break! With practice, you'll be a motherfucking lettering queen in no-time at all!

Here, I have broken down the lowercase letter "A" for you to see the individual strokes and how when they come together, they form the letter.

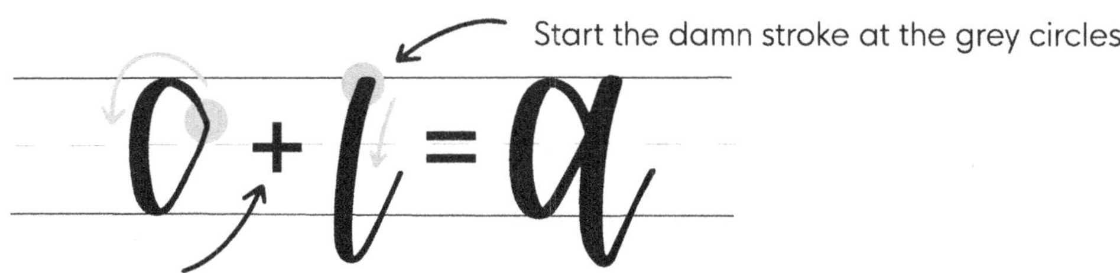

Pick up your pen at the end of the first fucking stroke

BASIC BITCH BRUSH ALPHABET: LOWERCASE

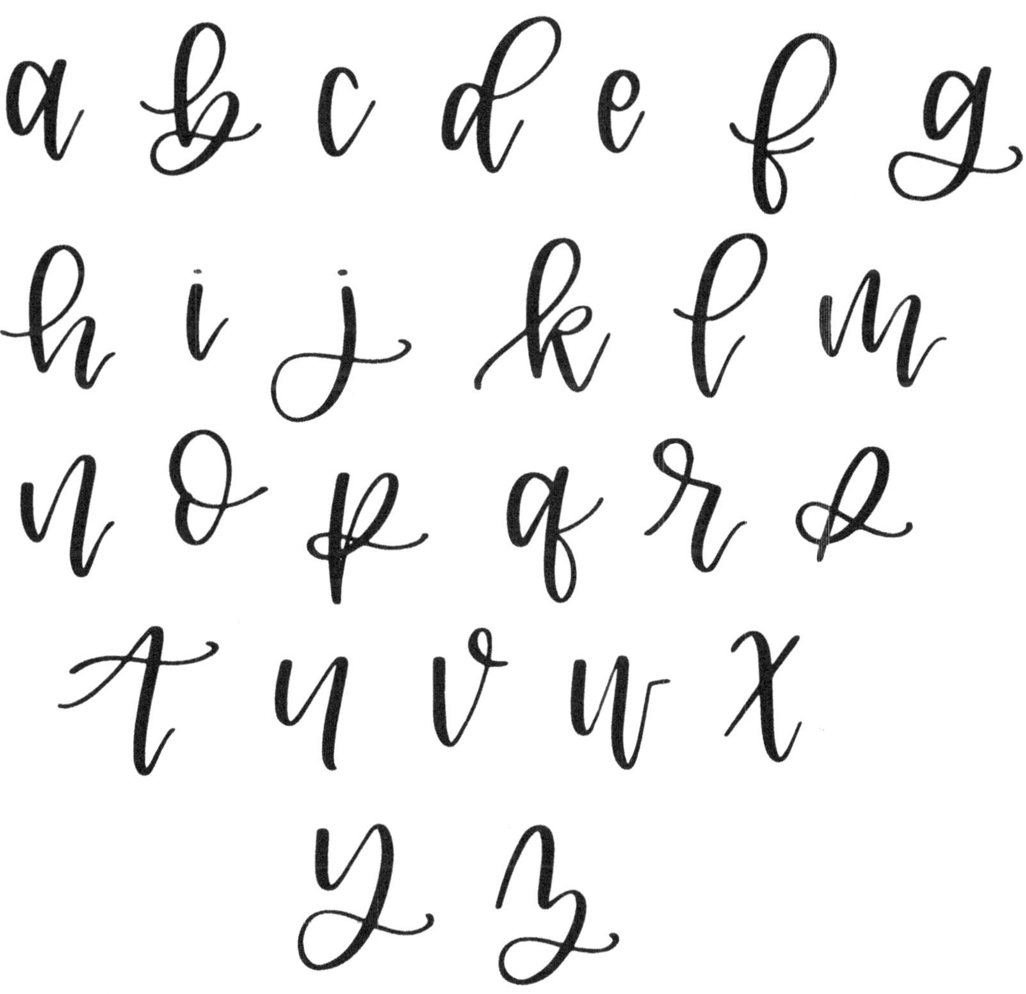

BASIC BITCH BRUSH ALPHABET

LOWERCASE

Use these damn great guidelines to practice your lettering by tracing them first. Sound good? Then, you can use the blank space to draw them yourself

a a a a

b b b b

c c c c

d d d d

e e e e

f f f f

g g g g

h h h h

BASIC BITCH BRUSH ALPHABET

LOWERCASE

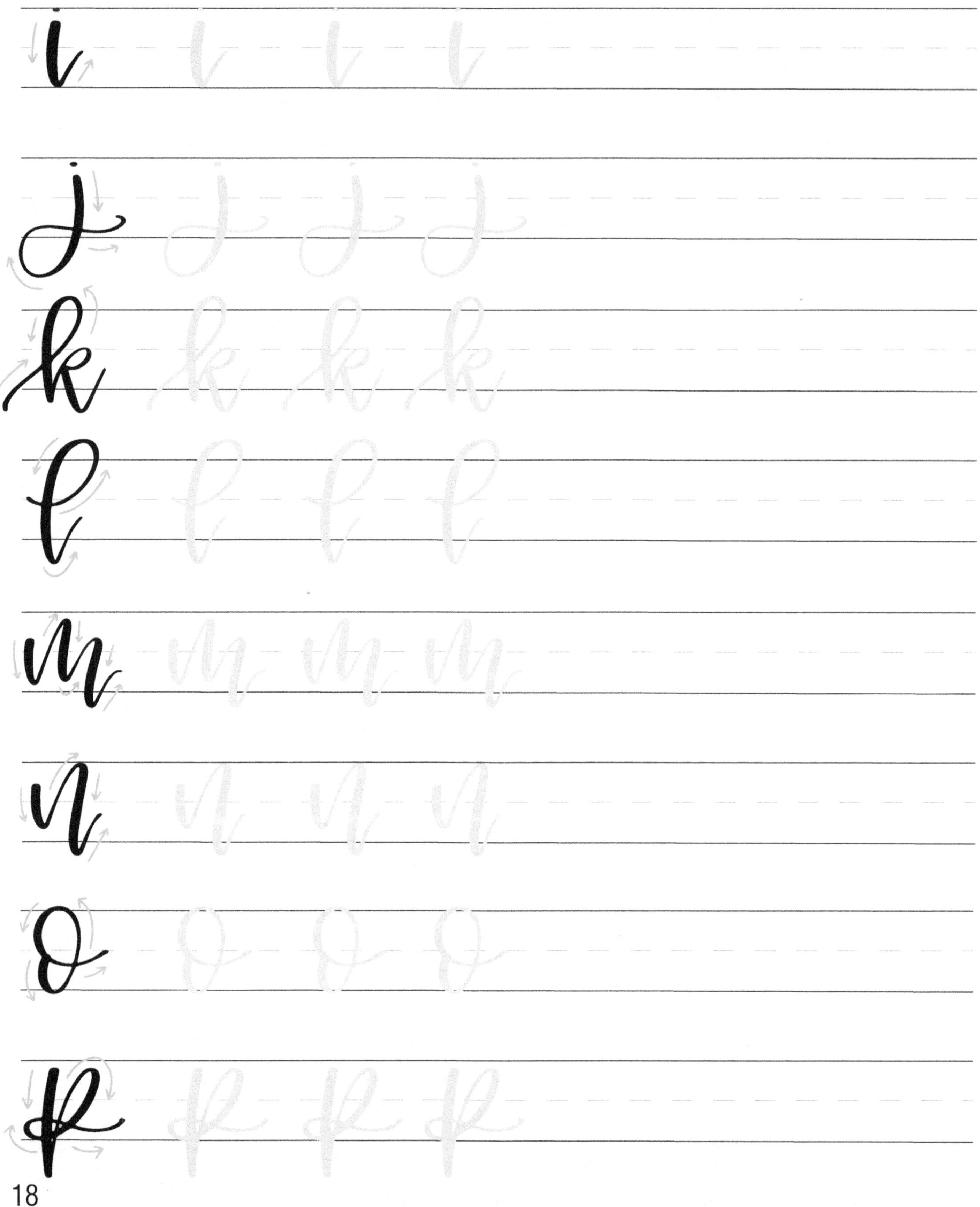

BASIC BITCH BRUSH ALPHABET

LOWERCASE

BASIC BITCH BRUSH ALPHABET

LOWERCASE

DON'T STOP FUCKING BELIEVING OR PRACTICING!

If you're going for the gold and need more practice than this, try using your brush pens on some premium laser jet paper. This kind of practice will make all other paper feel like shit. Once you use nice pens and paper – you'll never want to go back!

Looks
like it's
FUCK
this
SHIT
O'CLOCK

DON'T FORGET THIS SHIT! IT'S IMPORTANT!

☞ **Slow your fucking roll!** Even though it may seem that all of your` Instagram lettering idols are speedy as hell, they're not. They just film themselves in hyperlapse to make it look seamless and fast. The best in the lettering biz know that they have to take it slow if they want to make great shit!

☞ **Fucking lift your pen after each stroke.** There's no goddamn way to stress this point more. Always pick up your pen and think about your next stroke before you make it. Tbh, even the very fucking best letterers do this.

☞ **Practice. Practice. FUCKING PRACTICE!** Don't worry if your letters look a bit wonky and shitty at first, that's normal and you're totally on track to be a master letterer. After hours and hours of practicing – you're still going to suck a little. Keep practicing and keep your handy-dandy eraser near you as you keep doing your stroke and letter drills. Eventually all of this practice will make you a boss-ass lettering bitch!

☞ **Hard pressure for downstrokes, light pressure for upstrokes!**

BASIC BITCH BRUSH ALPHABET: UPPERCASE

A B C D E F G

H I J K L M

N O P Q R S

T U V W X

Y Z

BASIC BITCH BRUSH ALPHABET

UPPERCASE

First things first, use these guides to practice your letters and build up that sweet muscle memory. Then, once you're a fucking pro, you can practice drawing them yourself.

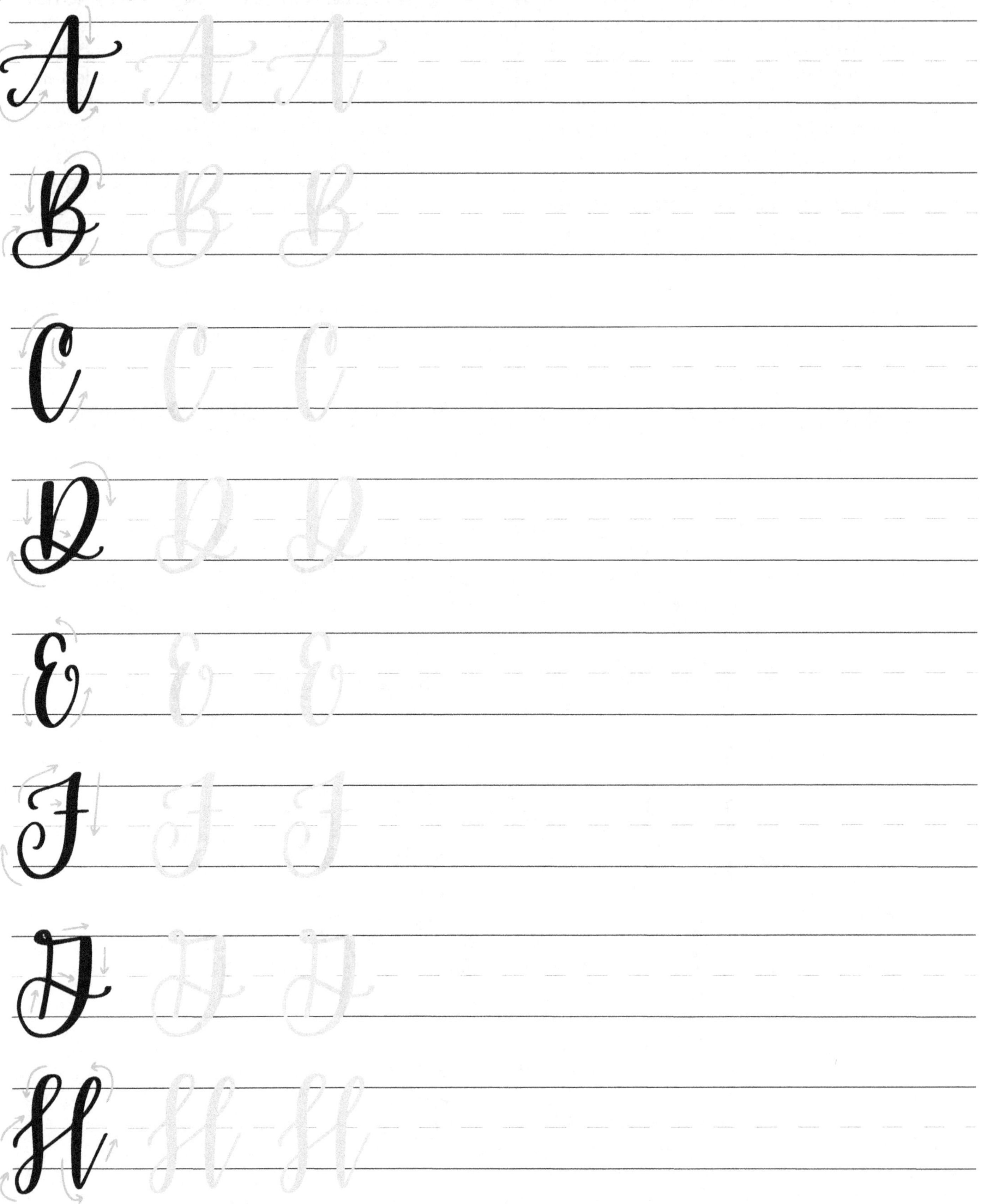

BASIC BITCH BRUSH ALPHABET

UPPERCASE

BASIC BITCH BRUSH ALPHABET

UPPERCASE

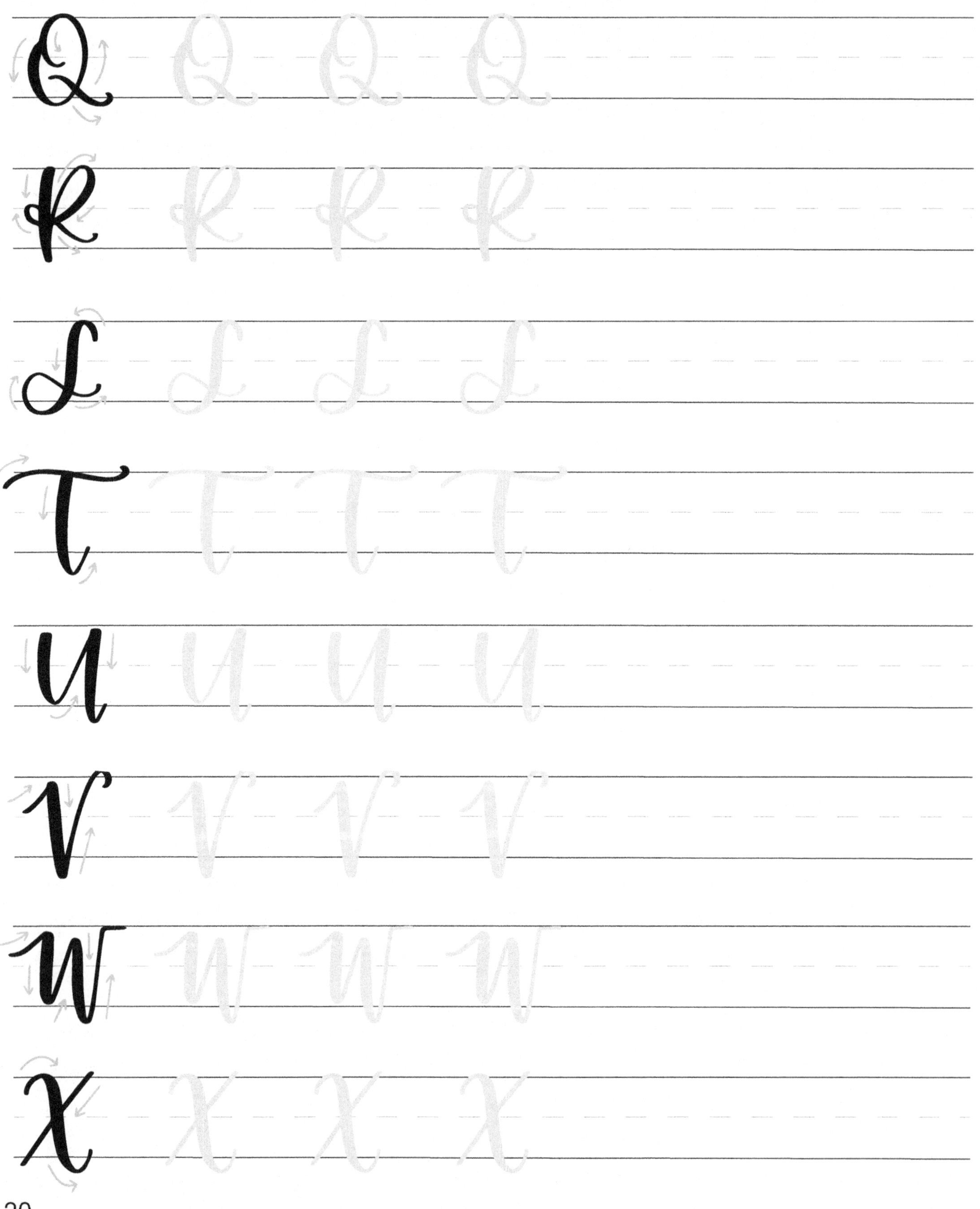

BASIC BITCH BRUSH ALPHABET

UPPERCASE

Y Y Y Y

Z Z Z Z

FREE YOUR FUCKING CREATIVE SOUL

There are many ways that are cool as hell to write some of these uppercase letters such as A,G, and Z. For example, A and G can be written in either of these fancy-ass ways:

A OR A G OR G

Try spicing things up by putting your own flair on these letters!

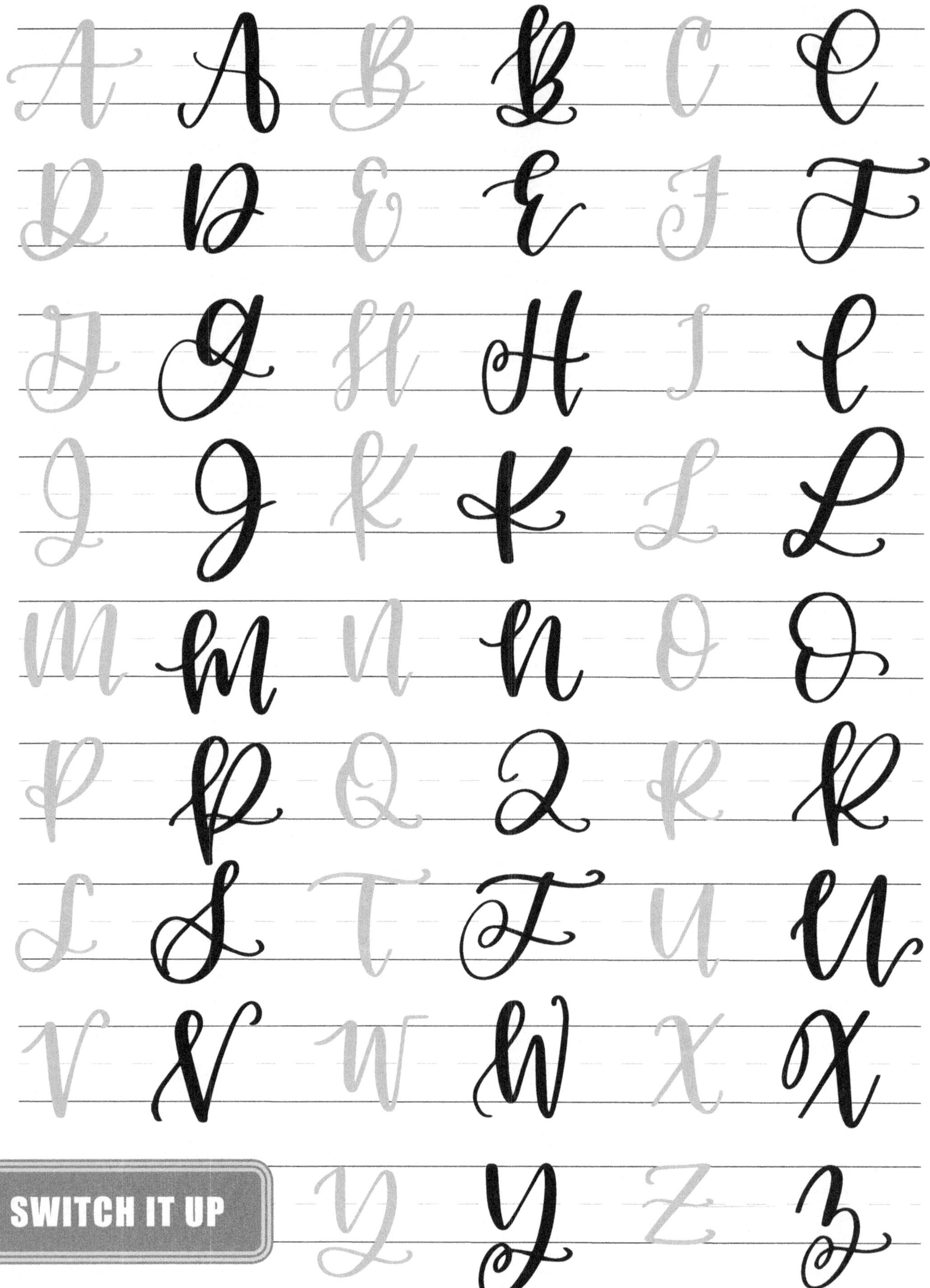

SWITCH IT UP

While the desire to achieve those beautiful brush lettered works of art was what originally got me interested in hand lettering, I quickly discovered the beauty of monoline lettering as well - and it soon became one of my favorite styles. If you remember from earlier in the book, you accomplish monoline lettering by using consistent pressure throughout the entire letter so that the width of your line is the same for all your strokes (no thick downstrokes and thin upstrokes here).

If you notice, this monoline alphabet is created using essentially the same letterforms as the Basic Brush Alphabet was - however the difference between monoline and brush lettering style results in an entirely different look.

The great thing about monoline lettering is that you can use any standard pen, pencil or marker with it. So put away those brush pens and pull out your favorite round tipped tool (I love using Micron pens or any pen designed for Monoline drawing). And again - a pencil works great here!

BASIC BITCH MONOLINE ALPHABET: LOWERCASE

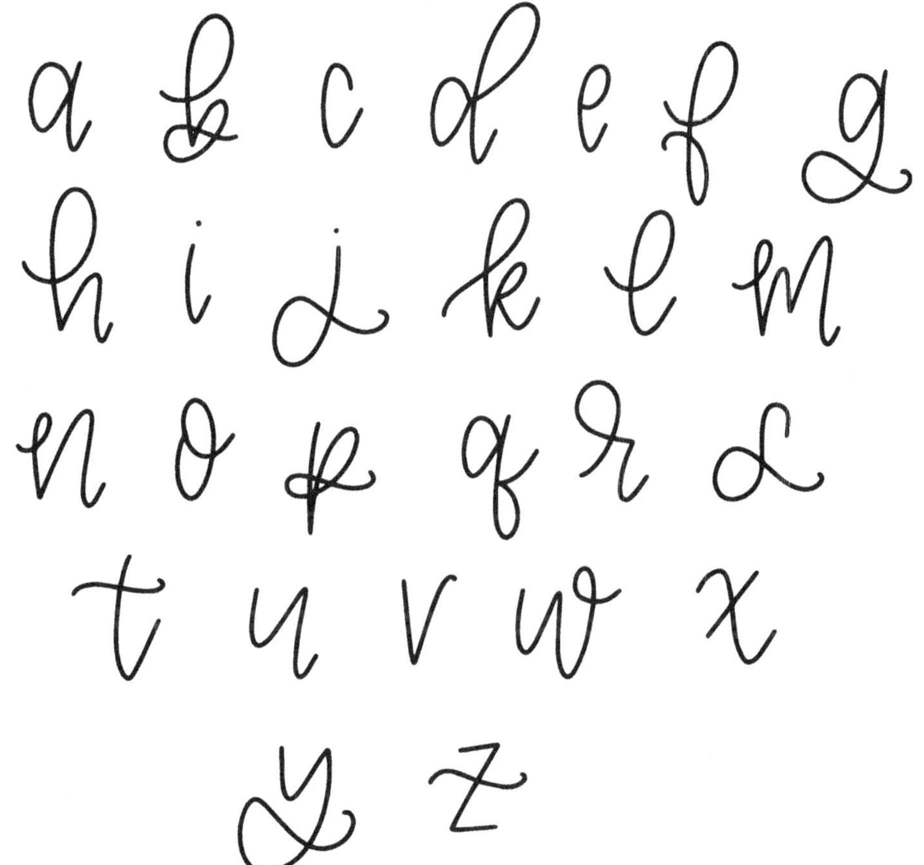

FAKE CALLIGRAPHY ESSENTIALS

Monoline lettering is great for creating faux calligraphy. To achieve this look, you simply draw your monoline letter or word, and then add a secondary line to each of your downstrokes and fill in the space between (or leave it open for a fun look all of its own!)

BASIC BITCH MONOLINE ALPHABET

LOWERCASE

Who said practice isn't fun? Try tracing the letters to give yourself a feel for your lettering style. Then, you can use the blank space to let yourself go nuts by drawing them yourself.

Attention: Don't fucking forget to pick up your pen after each and every stroke. Even those letters like "d" and "g" where it's hella tempting to do them in a single stroke. Don't. Do. It. Pick it up each and every time unless you want your lettering to turn out like shit.

WOO FAKE CALLIGRAPHY IS COOL AS HELL!

a

b

c

d

e

f

g

BASIC BITCH MONOLINE ALPHABET

LOWERCASE

WOO FAKE CALLIGRAPHY IS COOL AS HELL!

h

i

j

k

l

m

n

o

BASIC BITCH MONOLINE ALPHABET

LOWERCASE

WOO FAKE CALLIGRAPHY IS COOL AS HELL!

BASIC BITCH MONOLINE ALPHABET

LOWERCASE

x x x x

y y y y

z z z z

WOO FAKE CALLIGRAPHY IS COOL AS HELL!

X X X X

Y Y Y Y

Z Z Z Z

I'M A
RAY OF
Fucking
SUNSHINE

TRY THESE DOPE TIPS TO MAKE YOUR LETTERING THAT MUCH FUCKING BETTER:

1. If you believe – you can achieve...any style of lettering you can fucking imagine depending on the size of your pen. Pens that are broader look dope for chunky lettering, while thin and fine pens are perfect for that delicate and fancy look you're going for.
2. When lettering, you're going to develop a personal style for your swashes, flourishes and loops. But don't mix multiple styles otherwise your words are going to look kind of shitty and sloppy. As long as you stay fucking consistent, you'll be good!
3. Relax your damn hand! If you grip your pen or pencil too tightly you'll find that your hand will start to hurt and cramp up. If your grip it too tight it can actually make your lettering look shittier!

BASIC BITCH MONOLINE ALPHABET: UPPERCASE

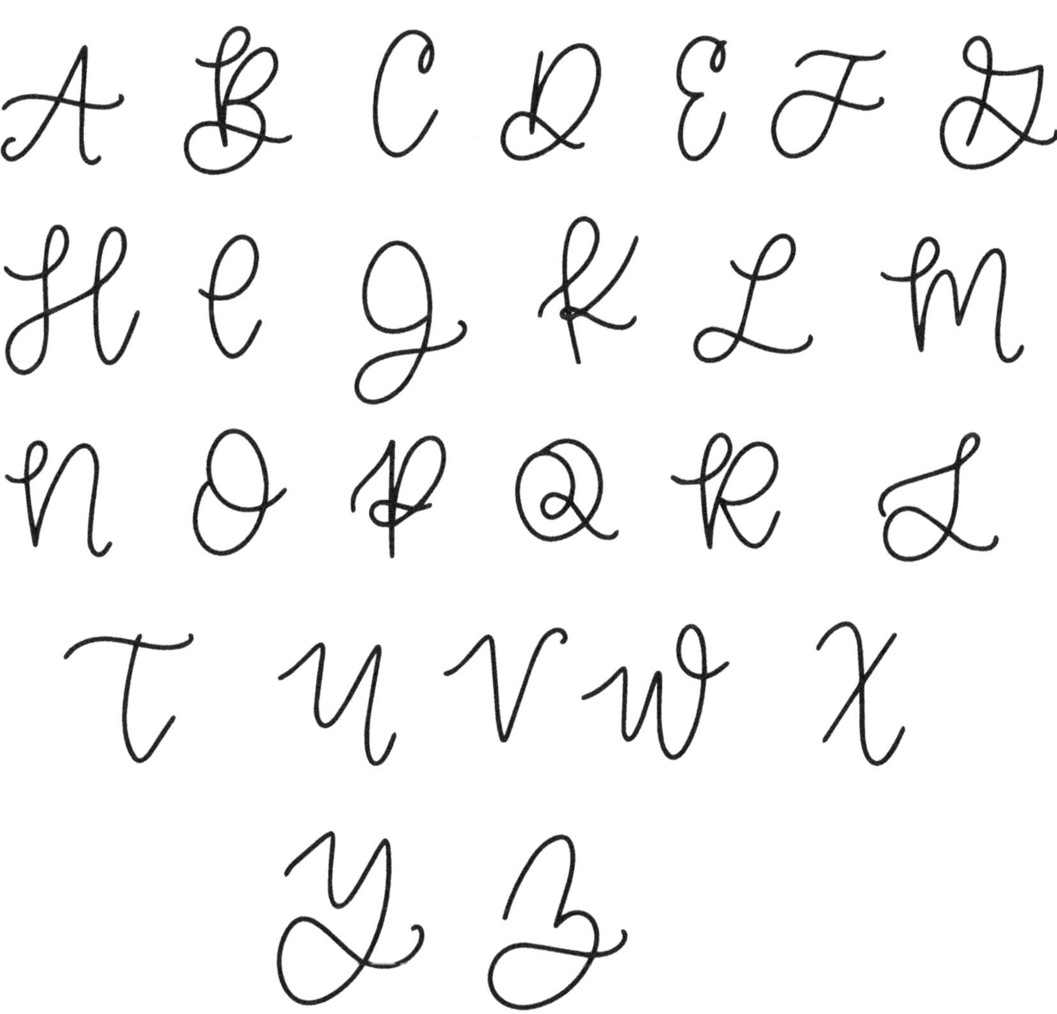

BASIC BITCH MONOLINE ALPHABET

UPPERCASE

Start out with tracing the letters for practice. Once you've done that, you can branch out to use the blank space to try them on your own.

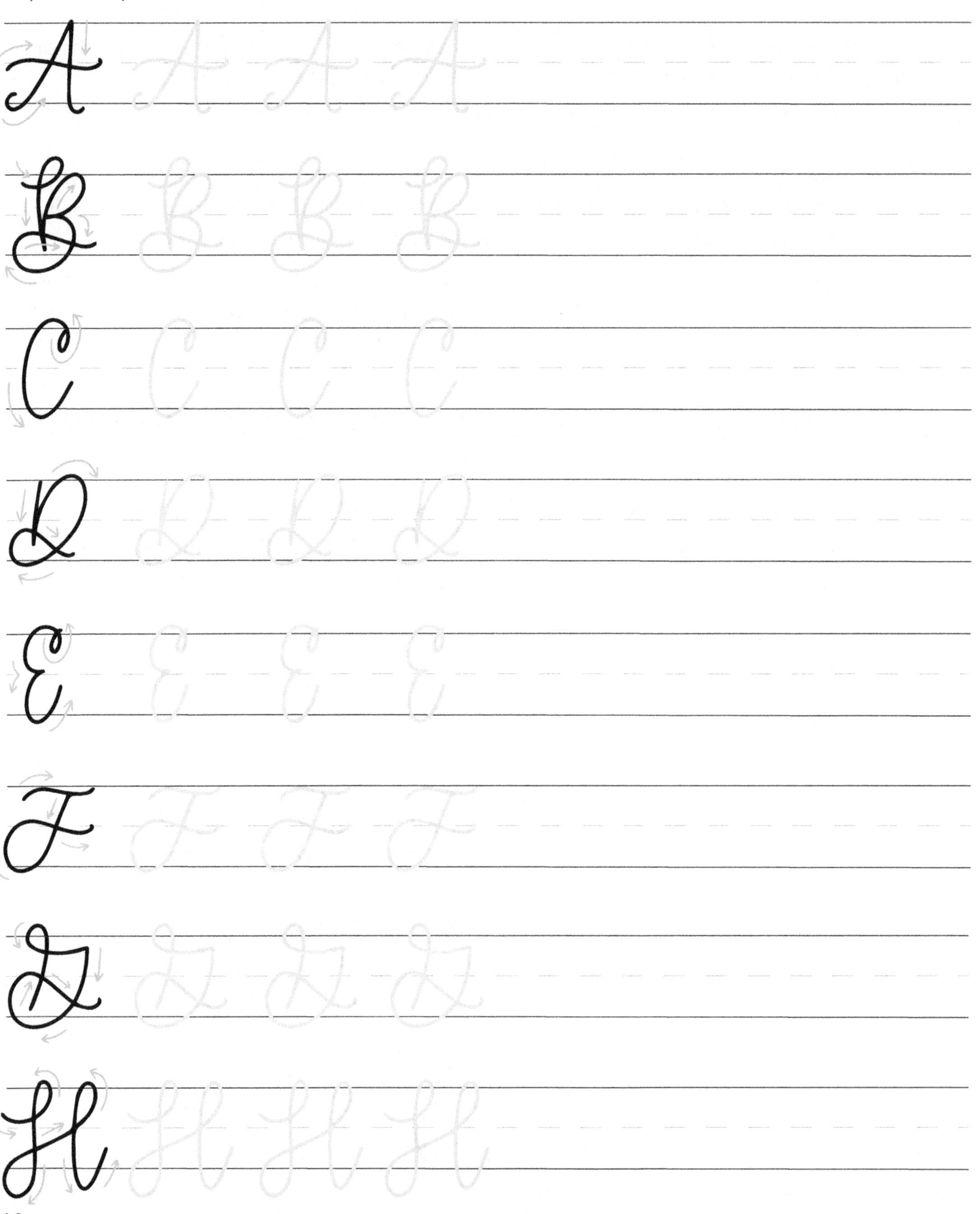

HELL YAH! LET'S DO SOME FAKE CALLIGRAPHY!

BASIC BITCH MONOLINE ALPHABET

UPPERCASE

HELL YAH! LET'S DO SOME FAKE CALLIGRAPHY!

BASIC BITCH MONOLINE ALPHABET

UPPERCASE

HELL YAH! LET'S DO SOME FAKE CALLIGRAPHY!

BASIC BITCH MONOLINE ALPHABET

UPPERCASE

HELL YAH! LET'S DO SOME FAKE CALLIGRAPHY!

VARIATIONS

CONNECTIONS AND WORDS

CONNECTING LETTERS TO MAKE SOME DAMN WORDS

So you're starting to do some fucking great work when drawing letters, but can you connect them?

Don't worry. You're a kickass letterer already and when you start connecting your letters they're not going to look like shit. All you have to do is pick up your pen at the end of each stroke and picture how you'll connnect it to the next letter. Damn, that makes it sound so easy. You'll find that after a while you'll naturally see how these damn letters connect and come together.

Here are a few examples to show the breakdown of the strokes as they form letters and are combined into words.

SHIT TO THINK ABOUT

- You're gonne be tempted to think that lettering is fucking easy like cursive. Well, no shit - it's not. Below is an example of a word written in cursive in one fluid motion, and a word that was lettered by hand. See how different they look?

- Before you even touch your pen to the goddamn paper, look at where you have the cross strokes and how you're gonna connect your letters. But the thing is, the letters don't need to be right fucking next to each other to make this happen.

- Finally, remember that you have some damn options when it comes to lettering. For example, if your letter has a descender, you can either give it a fancy-ass long tail or a flourish instead of having to connect it to the next letter. Just don't use too many fucking flourishes because it'll start to make things look shitty and complicated.

CONNECTING THOSE DAMN LETTERS

Hell yeah! It's practice time, baby! Go through these guides and practice connecting letters and then fucking try it yourself in the black space.

a b : ab ab

g r : gr gr

s w : sw sw

d o : do do

m i : mi mi

l a : la la

c h : ch ch

l l : ll ll

CONNECTING THOSE DAMN LETTERS

PRO TIP: make the "E" a little damn smaller and the "L" even bigger to keep them from looking too fucking similar.

GIVE THEM A FUCKING TRY YOURSELF!

hi :

pr :

st :

om :

bo :

Li :

qu :

ex :

BASIC BITCH LETTER WORDS

You know the drill, use the guide to practice and then take it away in the blank space! For this section, really strive to make your letters all cool as hell looking!

BASIC BITCH LETTER WORDS

ass ass

bastard bastard

bitches bitches

smartass smartass

salty salty

woke woke

shit shit

fuckity fuckity

BASIC BITCH LETTER WORDS

basic basic

slay slay

mofo mofo

thirsty thirsty

hunty hunty

no fucks no fucks

snarky snarky

shade shade

BASIC MONOLINE LETTER WORDS

dope as hell dope as hell

crazy shit crazy shit

total prick total prick

bitch bitch

dumbass dumbass

fuck you fuck you

my bitches my bitches

Shit happens Shit happens

BASIC MONOLINE LETTER WORDS

sassy sassy

sweary sweary

ghost ghost

motherfucker motherfucker

ratchet ratchet

fuck it fuck it

bastards bastards

damn it damn it

BASIC MONOLINE LETTER WORDS

kickass kickass

awesome awesome

baller baller

hella cool hella cool

dope dope

shook shook

fancy fancy

savage savage

Fuck
BAD
Vibes

VARIATIONS AND ILLUSTRATIONS

SERIF ALPHABET

A B C D E F G H I

J K L M N O P Q R

S T U V W X Y Z

a b c d e f g h i

j k l m n o p q r

s t u v w x y z

SAN SERIF ALPHABET

A B C D E F G H I

J K L M N O P Q R

S T U V W X Y Z

a b c d e f g h i

j k l m n o p q r

s t u v w x y z

MAKE SOME DAMN VARIATIONS

With limitless ways you can make each letter your bitch, you can really create a style that's all your own. After spending your time practicing each damn technique over and over, it's finally time for your to let loose and do your own thing. What the hell! Go crazy and make some variations!

It sucks to hear it, but thinking about each letter or each word individually isn't enough to make beautiful fucking lettering. You'll have to think about how to fill the empty spaces between letters, words, or even in the surrounding area. Here are some ways you can kick your lettering up a damn knotch!

 The first thing you need to do is switch up your swashes. Now try saying that 5 times fast. By adding some sick loops, curving your swash in different ways, or even getting rid of the damn thing can help you add some style to your lettering!

 Next, make your letters a little bit bouncier. Don't know what the fuck that means? Well, you basically just have the bowls, eyes, and curves in your letters bigger and rounder while adding some curvy-ass flourishes!

 Another way to spice up your lettering is to create a ligature with your cross strokes between letters. Basically, use your cross stroke of one letter to lead into another letter. It looks cool as hell.

 Make sure that you're flexible with how you put your letters on the baseline. Switch up the sizes of some of your letters to give them a signature look. But don't make them too differently sized because they'll look like shit when strung together in a word.

 Finally, throw in some flourishes – but not too many, bitch! Flourishes can make your lettering look fun and unique, but if you put in too many it can all go to hell pretty quickly.

SWITCH SHIT UP

Changing things up with your font styles is one of the best fucking parts of lettering! You can be a bad bitch and try out a variety of font styles until you find a combination that works for you.

Check out some of these bomb-ass combinations for you to try out!

Basic Brush
SKINNY SAN SERIF

UPPERCASE SAN SERIF
bold monoscript

monoscript
UPPERCASE SERIF

Want to make your lettering look extra dope? Add a flourish wherever! You can put it at the beginning or end of the word and try out using an ascender, decender, or cross stroke.

For some bitches, flourishes can be the hardest part of lettering to get the hang of. The best way to master them is by simply practing flourishes over and over until you find a style that's hella comfortable for you. Keep trying, bitch!

1. A tip to keep flourishes looking great is by loosening the grip on your pen, pencil, or brush. If your grip to too tight, your flourishes are going to look messy and shaky.

2. Bitch, the only way you're going to get better is if you keep practicing. You're going to do PLENTY of flourishes that look wonky or weird. Don't fucking give up! Push through and keep practicing.

3. The last thing to remember is don't go fucking crazy with flourishes. If you include too many it can look complicated and hella hard to read. Everything in moderation, including alcohol and flourishes.

FLOURISHES AND SWASHES

Now it's time to put brush/pen/pencil/whatever to paper and practice those damn flourishes! When you're done using the guides, try using the blank space to try your own fucking flourishes.

fucking fucking

shit shit

hell hell

damn damn

squad squad

shitty shitty

thirsty thirsty

thicc thicc

hangry hangry

bougie bougie

BOTANICAL LINE DRAWINGS

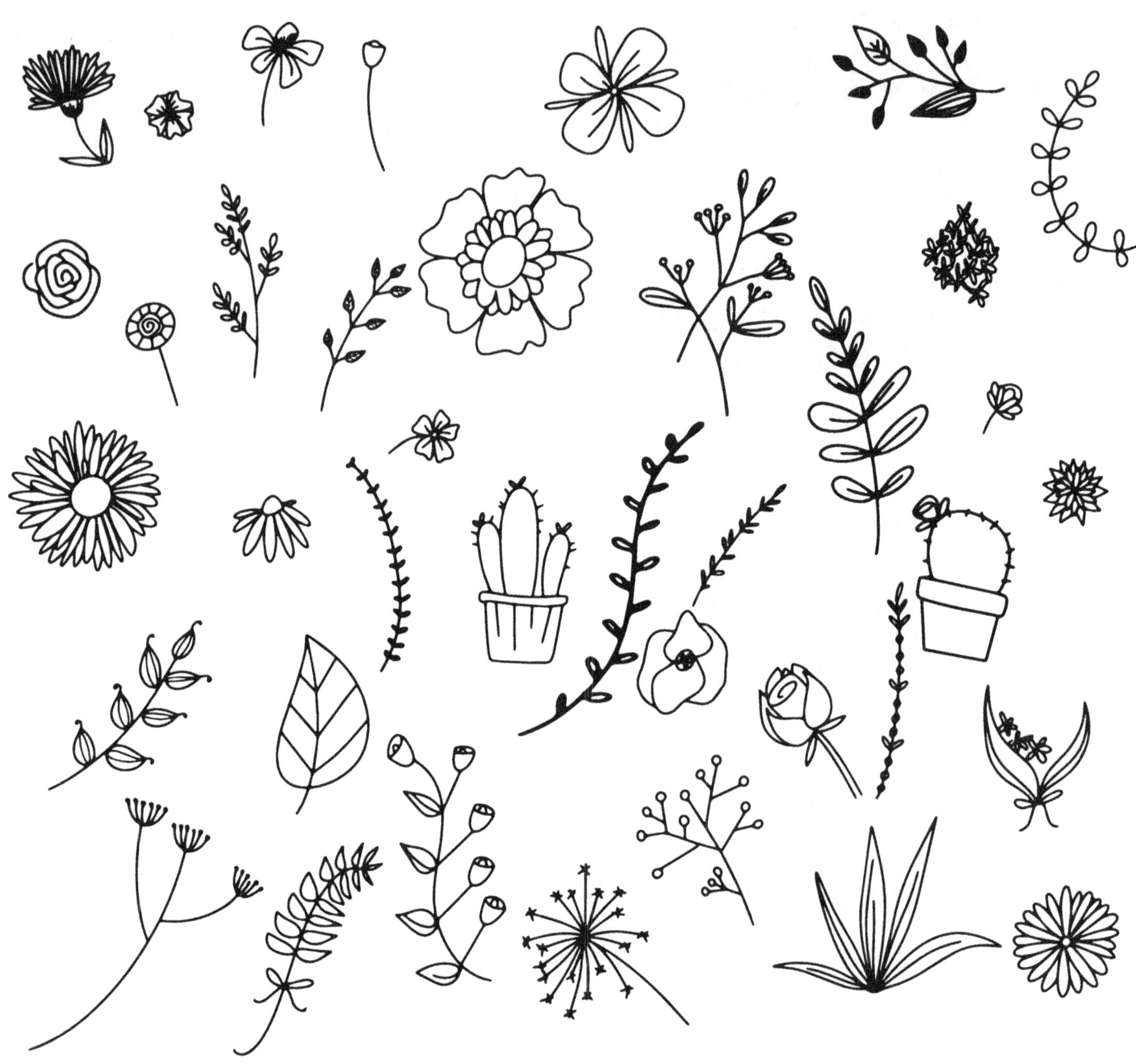

Take your lettering pieces to the next fucking level with some botanical additions. Wondering what the hell you're going to do with all of that empty-ass space around your lettering? Add some bonatical elements. Problem fucking solved.

RIBBONS AND BANNERS

TIPS AND TRICKS TO PIMP YOUR BANNER

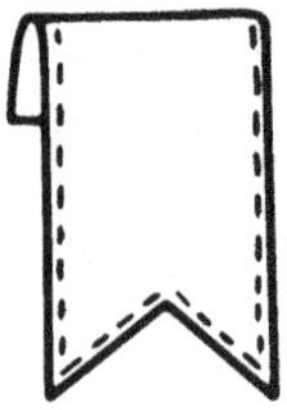

Adding some sweetass accents to your ribbons and banners will really give them the extra « oopmh » they need.

Try out some different techniques to see what you like. For example, thin paralell lines, stippling, and cross hatches will give your shadows some fucking depth!

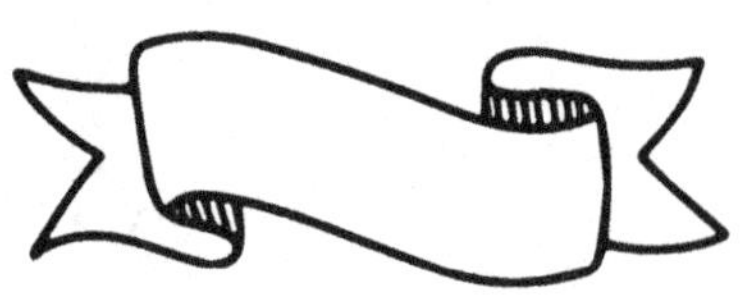

Pro tip! If you can't figure out what to add to your lettering and you're in a fucking creative funk, just make a list of random object. Then, start doodling your own version of those objects. It's a great way to add some fucking flair and whimsy to your lettering.

CARPE
THAT
Fucking
DIEM

DESIGN COMPOSITION

FINISHING YOUR DAMN WORK

Con-fucking-gratulations! You're already at the final step in your lettering journey – creating a hand lettered design. Basically, this means you will take everything your ass has learned and put it all together!

Remember that all of these damn lettering suggestions are just that – suggestions. In the end, get crazy and creative when coming up with ways to design your own lettering pieces.

Here are two quick and easy-ass steps for you to keep in mind when you're creating a finished piece.

First, you need to write down the phrase on some scrap paper. This can help you figure out which fucking words are the most important and where you want the ascenders, descenders, and cross strokes to be. All of this planning will prevent your final piece from looking like shit!

After that, lightly sketch out the focus words in pencil on your final paper. You want these words to really fucking pop off of the page and stand out the most. Use super light pressure when sketching so you don't accidentally make any indentations. Got that, bitch?

After sketching out your focus words, you can figure out how the fuck you're going to fit the rest of the words into the design. Make sure you're paying damn close attention to the placement so it's hella easy to read.

Next, have your ass start sketching all of the florals, doodles or illustrations that you want to fill the negative space. Just make sure they fit the vibe of your piece and don't look shitty or random.

5

Now that you've gotten everything drawn out in pencil, you can start using your ink. Depending on the fucking vibe you're going for, you might want to choose either your brush pen or monoline pen. Don't worry if your inking doesn't abso-fucking-lutely line up with your pencil, you can always go back and erase later.

And – BAM – now you've got this amazing looking finished fucking design!

Now, the time has finally fucking come for you to try lettering some composed pieces. Below are eight damn simple hand lettered designs for you to use for practice on.

Most importantly – have fucking fun with this bitch! After a while of trying out different styles and techniques you'll find that your lettering will turn out hella amazing.

FINAL DESIGN

WELL SHIT

Practice fucking tracing the design by focusing your shit on the primary words first, then the remaining words, and ending with the damn doodles.

NOW, TRY IT AND DO IT WITHOUT ANY DAMN HELP!

FINALLY, IT'S TIME TO LET YOUR FREAK FLAG FUCKING FLY AND LETTER IT IN YOUR OWN PERSONAL STYLE!

FINAL DESIGN

NOBODY CARES

Practice fucking tracing the design by focusing your shit on the primary words first, then the remaining words, and ending with the damn doodles.

NOW, TRY IT AND DO IT WITHOUT ANY DAMN HELP!

FINALLY, IT'S TIME TO LET YOUR FREAK FLAG FUCKING FLY AND LETTER IT IN YOUR OWN PERSONAL STYLE!

FINAL DESIGN

WELCOME TO THE SHIT SHOW

Practice fucking tracing the design by focusing your shit on the primary words first, then the remaining words, and ending with the damn doodles.

welcome
TO THE
shit show!

welcome
TO THE
shit show!

NOW, TRY IT AND DO IT WITHOUT ANY DAMN HELP!

FINALLY, IT'S TIME TO LET YOUR FREAK FLAG FUCKING FLY AND LETTER IT IN YOUR OWN PERSONAL STYLE!

FINAL DESIGN

WHAT THE ACTUAL FUCK

Practice fucking tracing the design by focusing your shit on the primary words first, then the remaining words, and ending with the damn doodles.

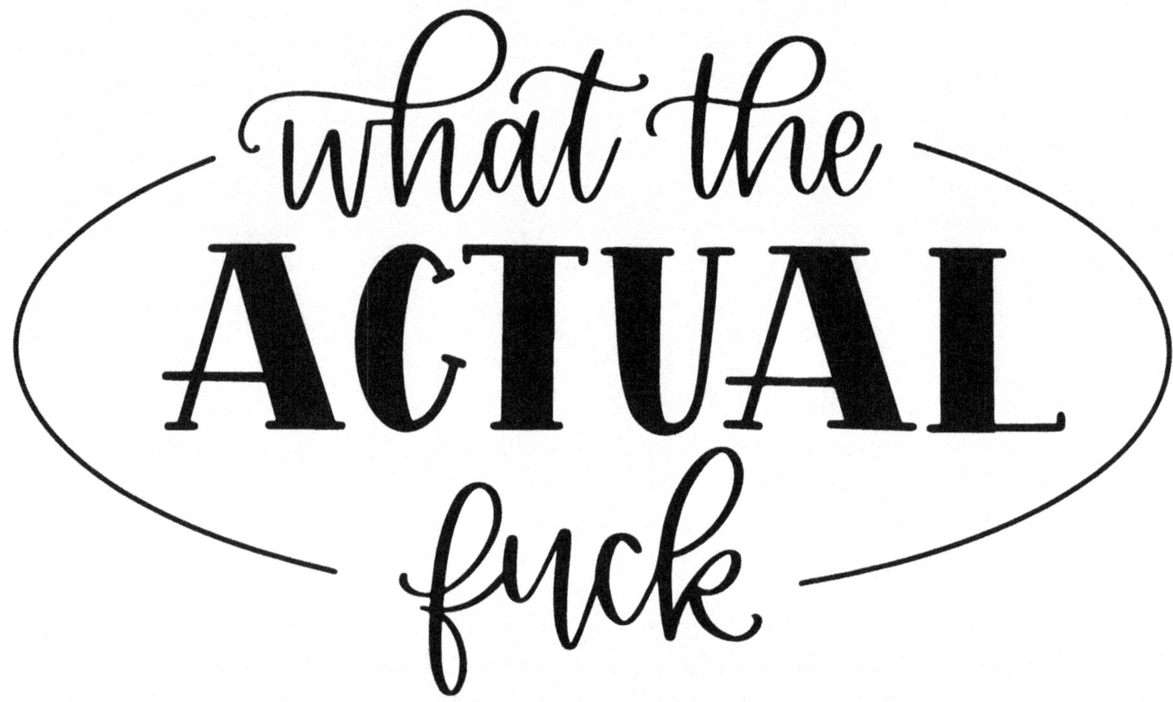

what the
ACTUAL
fuck

NOW, TRY IT AND DO IT WITHOUT ANY DAMN HELP!

FINALLY, IT'S TIME TO LET YOUR FREAK FLAG FUCKING FLY AND LETTER IT IN YOUR OWN PERSONAL STYLE!

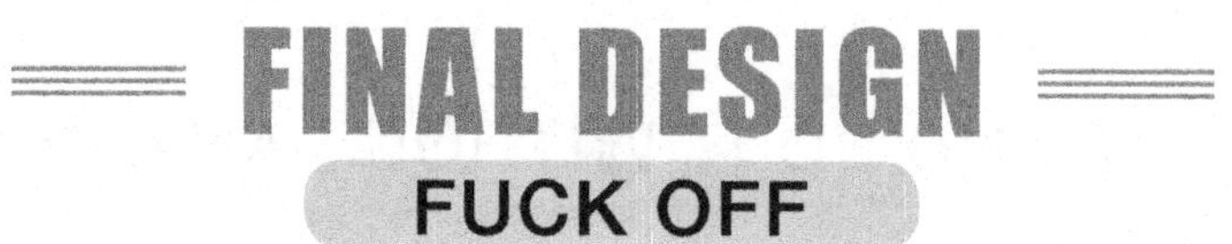

Practice fucking tracing the design by focusing your shit on the primary words first, then the remaining words, and ending with the damn doodles.

NOW, TRY IT AND DO IT WITHOUT ANY DAMN HELP!

FINALLY, IT'S TIME TO LET YOUR FREAK FLAG FUCKING FLY AND LETTER IT IN YOUR OWN PERSONAL STYLE!

FINAL DESIGN

FUCKITY FUCK, FUCK, FUCK

Practice fucking tracing the design by focusing your shit on the primary words first, then the remaining words, and ending with the damn doodles.

NOW, TRY IT AND DO IT WITHOUT ANY DAMN HELP!

FINALLY, IT'S TIME TO LET YOUR FREAK FLAG FUCKING FLY AND LETTER IT IN YOUR OWN PERSONAL STYLE!

Practice fucking tracing the design by focusing your shit on the primary words first, then the remaining words, and ending with the damn doodles.

NOW, TRY IT AND DO IT WITHOUT ANY DAMN HELP!

FINALLY, IT'S TIME TO LET YOUR FREAK FLAG FUCKING FLY AND LETTER IT IN YOUR OWN PERSONAL STYLE!

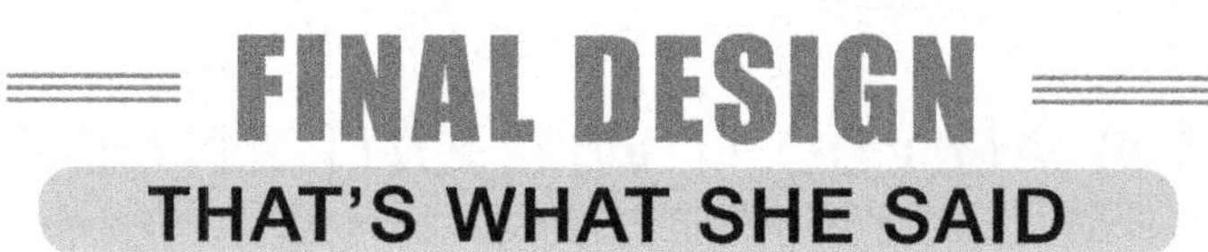

FINAL DESIGN

THAT'S WHAT SHE SAID

Practice fucking tracing the design by focusing your shit on the primary words first, then the remaining words, and ending with the damn doodles.

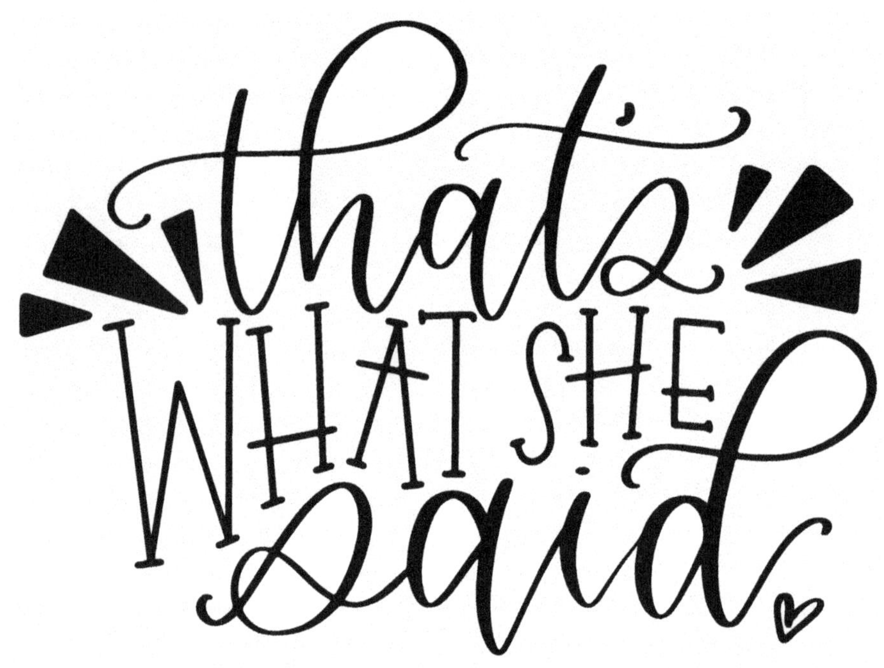

NOW, TRY IT AND DO IT WITHOUT ANY DAMN HELP!

FINALLY, IT'S TIME TO LET YOUR FREAK FLAG FUCKING FLY AND LETTER IT IN YOUR OWN PERSONAL STYLE!

Made in the USA
Coppell, TX
15 March 2021

51758673R00059